You're in the Band

Book 2

Unplugged

For Acoustic Guitar
by Dave Clo

Includes Online Audio

PLAYBACK+
Speed • Pitch • Balance • Loop

Each song includes two audio tracks: one at a manageable rehearsal tempo, and the other at a faster performance tempo.
With our exclusive **PLAYBACK+** feature, you can change the tempo even more without altering the pitch,
plus set loop points for continuous repetition of tricky measures.

To access audio, visit:
www.halleonard.com/mylibrary

Enter Code
6507-6248-1419-7348

Recording Musicians:

DAVE CLO – Guitars, Bass, and Keyboards
CHRIS DAUPHIN – Additional Keyboards
TIM CLO – Drums

Cover Photography by Matt Taylor
Adplate photos used by permission of **jj@astartledchameleon.co.uk**

ISBN 978-0-87718-070-8

WILLIS MUSIC

EXCLUSIVELY DISTRIBUTED BY

HAL•LEONARD®

7777 W. BLUEMOUND RD. P.O. BOX 13819
MILWAUKEE, WISCONSIN 53213

Visit Hal Leonard Online at
www.halleonard.com

Contact us:
Hal Leonard
7777 West Bluemound Road
Milwaukee, WI 53213
Email: info@halleonard.com

In Europe, contact:
Hal Leonard Europe Limited
42 Wigmore Street
Marylebone, London, W1U 2RN
Email: info@halleonardeurope.com

In Australia, contact:
Hal Leonard Australia Pty. Ltd.
4 Lentara Court
Cheltenham, Victoria, 3192 Australia
Email: info@halleonard.com.au

2   **Congratulations!** We've talked it over and decided that "You're In the Band!"

Here is a list of the songs you will need to learn. When you can play your part with the rehearsal track without any mistakes, write the date mastered to the right of the rehearsal track space. When you have perfected a song with the performance track, write in that date too. GET BUSY! We have our first show in about six months!

 Whenever this icon appears, that means that there are audio tracks that you can stream or download online using the special code on the first page.

SONG INDEX

Page	Title	Date Rehearsal Track Mastered	Date Performance Track Mastered
6	Rock-E	_____	_____
7	Grunge-E	_____	_____
8	Effigy	_____	_____
9	E-Mail	_____	_____
10	Two Down	_____	_____
11	Besieged	_____	_____
12	2nd Stringer	_____	_____
13	Phrygian Sea	_____	_____
14	The Gauge	_____	_____
15	Ice Age	_____	_____
16	Spare	_____	_____
17	Graduation	_____	_____
18	Geology	_____	_____
20	Forthright?	_____	_____
21	Delivery	_____	_____
22	Staircase	_____	_____
23	Pentatonic	_____	_____
24	Adrian	_____	_____
25	Out on a Ledger	_____	_____
26	5th Wheel	_____	_____
27	A Minor Setback	_____	_____
28	Rock-E VI	_____	_____
29	Surf String	_____	_____
30	Octavee	_____	_____
31	Upshot	_____	_____

INTRODUCTION

   The songs in Book 2 are more advanced melodies (solos) set to the same music as in Book 1. If you have a friend that plays guitar, you can play both solos from Book 1 and 2 together. Another practice idea is to play the solo from one book while listening to the rehearsal track of the other book.

   Some of the new songs may seem too difficult at first. Remember that the best way to master a new piece is to break it down into smaller sections, memorize the individual parts, and then put it all together. *It is very important for a musician to develop the ability to memorize.*

   Don't worry if it feels like you are not getting better at reading music. *Learn the songs any way that you can*...by memorizing parts...using your ear...or even seeing pictures that the notes seem to draw. Any trick that works for you is OK because everyone's brain works differently.

   The most important thing is that you learn to *play the songs correctly, in time and with feeling.* Eventually the reading will get easier. Oh yeah...Don't forget to have **FUN!**

THE BASICS

Important Stuff From Book 1

The BASICS you should know from Book 1 before continuing with Book 2:

The Staff, Bar Lines, Measures, Treble Clef, Common Time, Whole Notes,
Half Notes, Quarter Notes, 8th Notes, Dotted Half Notes and Final Bar Lines.
----- *See Book 1, page 5 for a description of these items* -----

Tuning the Guitar

You can tune: with the online tuning track (each string is played 3 times)

with a piano   or

to the guitar itself   (see Book 1, page 4)

Playing 8th Notes

Remember that 1, 2, 3 and 4
are played with down-picks ⊓
while the &'s are up-picks ∨
(This is the general rule, there are exceptions)

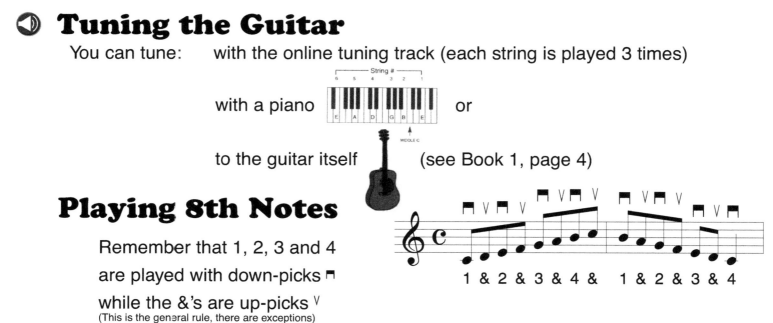

1 & 2 & 3 & 4 &   1 & 2 & 3 & 4

8 More Things To Know From Book 1

Pick-up Notes, B Flat (♭), Rests: (Whole, Half, Quarter and 8th),
Fermata, Ledger Lines, Ties, Octaves and Repeat Sign.

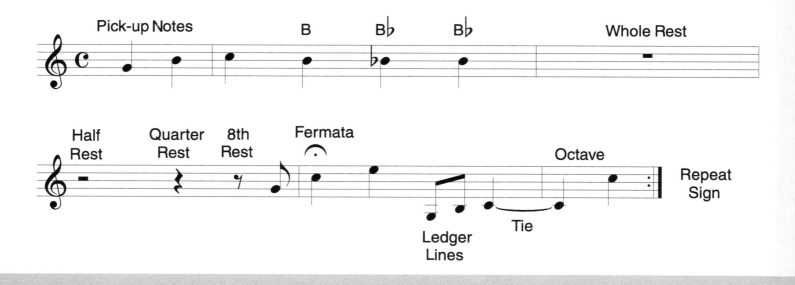

The Notes

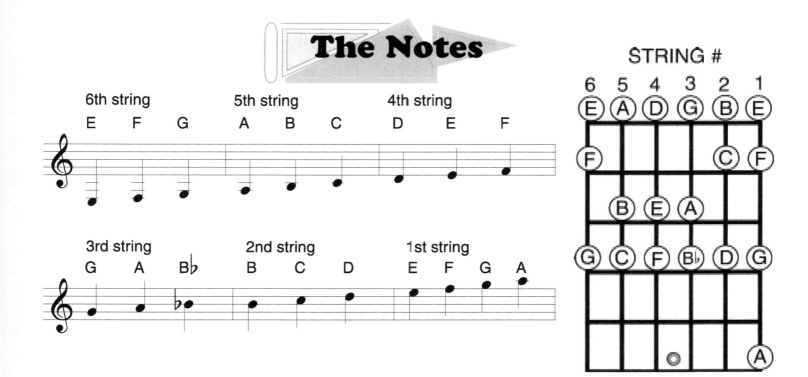

Reviewing the Dot

The Dot placed next to a note increases the time value of the note by 1/2. For example:

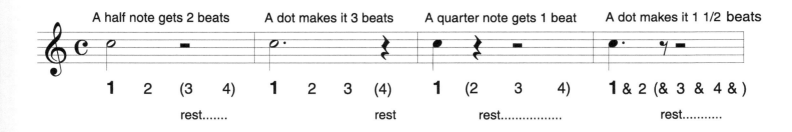

More with the Dot
(you won't need to know this stuff for a while)

With the rest first   8th notes are 1/2 beat each (2 for 1 beat)   Dotted 8ths need a 16th note to make 1 beat

(1) **&** 2 & (3)   4   **1**   **&** (2) **&** 3 (&   4)   **1** e **&** **a** (2)   **3** e **&** a (4)

LOTS OF 8TH NOTES

A steady stream of 8th notes is actually easier to read than a rhythm that mixes it up more. The first 4 songs may have a lot of notes, but the rhythms should be simple to read.

To make things easier..

Take note of how many times a measure is repeated.
- Put a small 1 above all the measures that are the same as the first measure.
- Put a 2 over all measures that are repeats of the next measure and so on.

You will be surprised how few measures need to be practiced.

ROCK-E

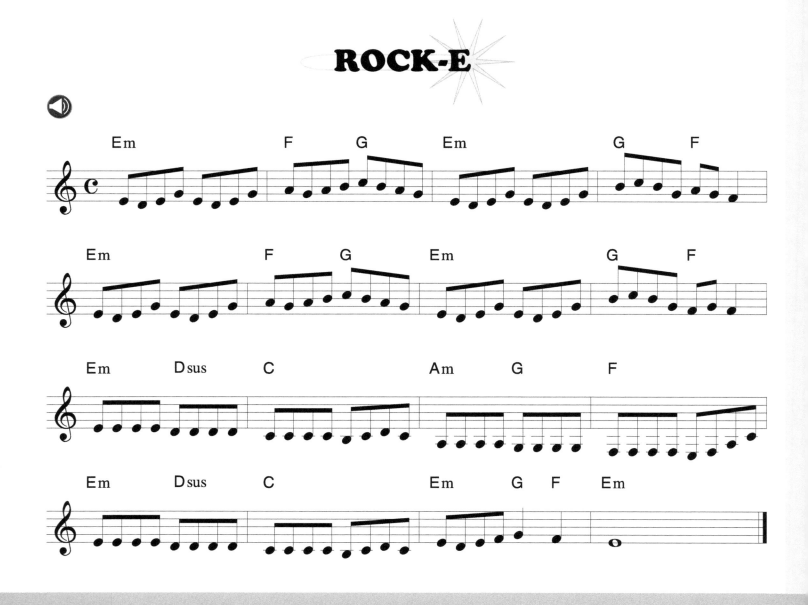

As mentioned in Book 1, recognizing patterns is the easiest way to learn, memorize and read music. Here are some patterns named to look like their shape. Use the blank staves on the next page to name your own patterns.

Patterns:

Mountain - (skip up, skip down)

or

Big Mountain - (skip up, skip up, skip down, skip down)

Valley - (skip down, skip up)

or

Big Valley - (skip down, skip down, skip up, skip up)

GRUNG-E

YOUR PATTERNS

Fact File

The **double bar line** is used to show the end of a section of music.
In this song, the **double bar line** shows the half-way point of the piece.
Note: the 1st half and 2nd half are almost identical.

EFFIGY

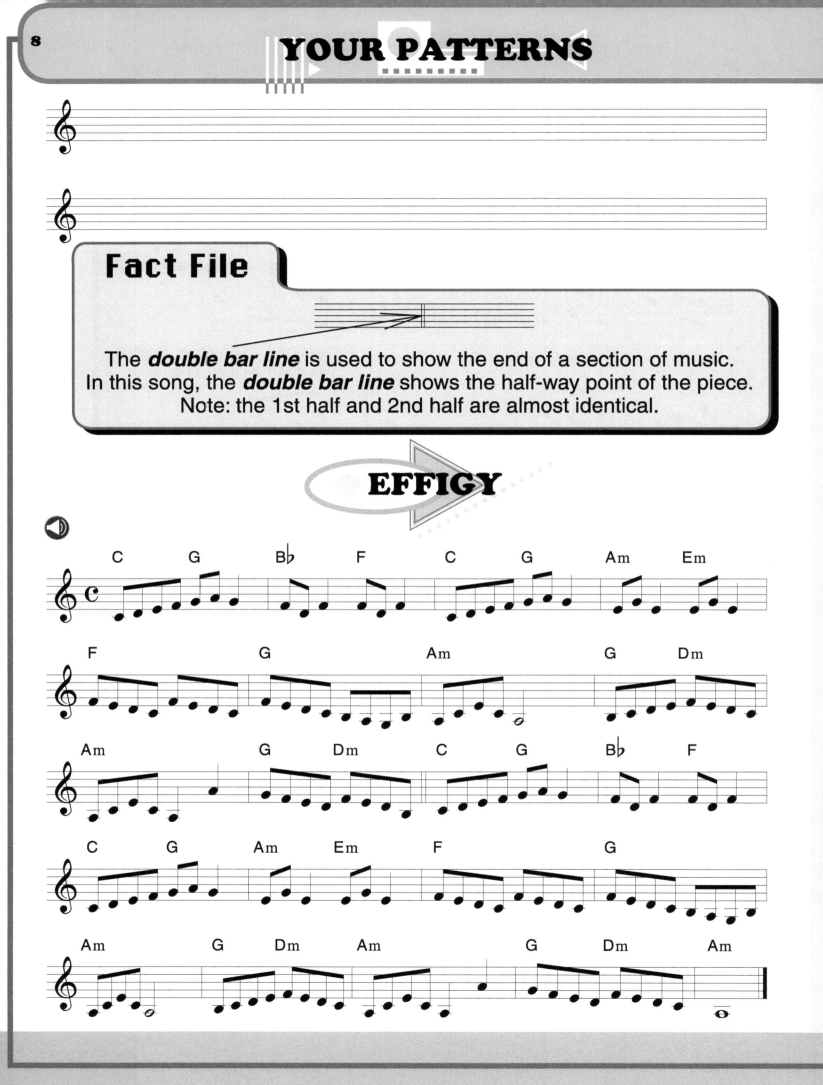

Patterns:

Rolling Hills - (Connected notes going up and down)

Find the low and high notes, then connect them with all the notes in between.

Notice that in lines *1,2,5* and *6* there is only one *"skip"*. All other notes are connecting.

E-MAIL

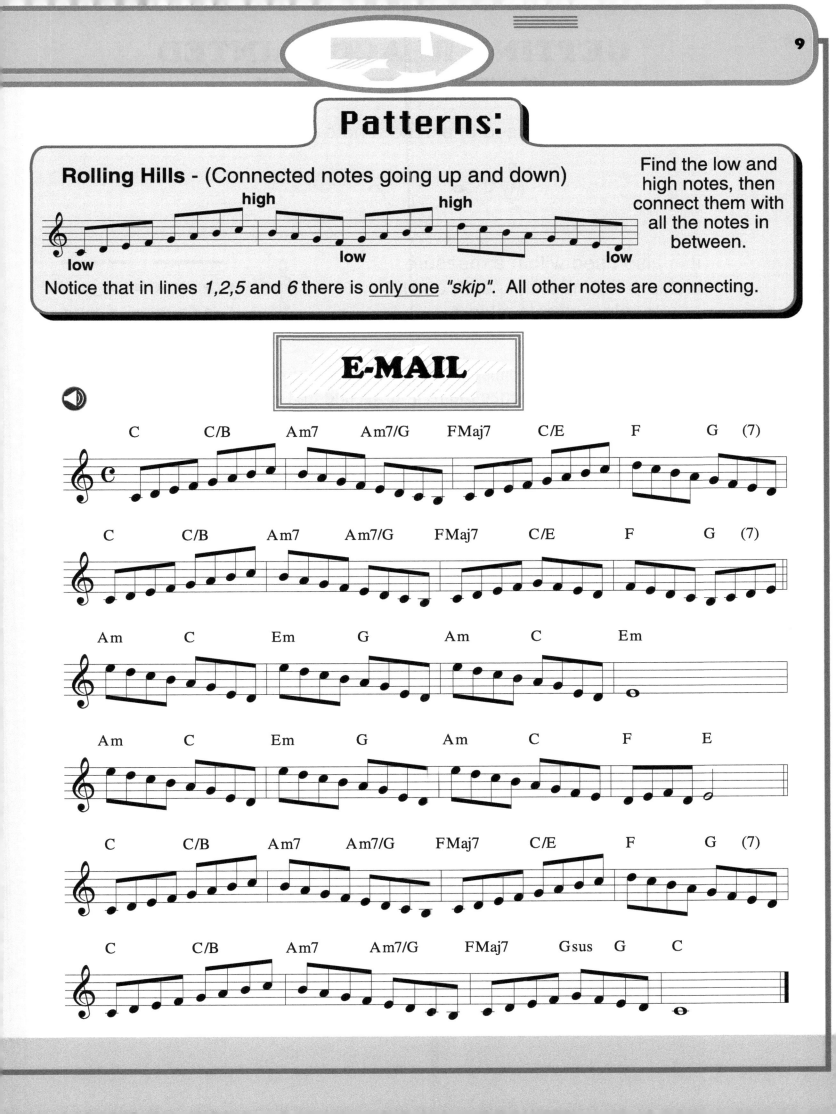

GETTING REACQUAINTED WITH THE "TIE"

A **tie** is <u>NOT</u> only used to extend a note into the next measure:

It is also used within a measure
to skip a downbeat (1, 2, 3, or 4).
In this example, skip 4.

The upcoming rhythms may be difficult to read, so make sure you listen to how they sound on the rehearsal track and memorize them. You will find that they are not as hard to play as they look.

TWO DOWN

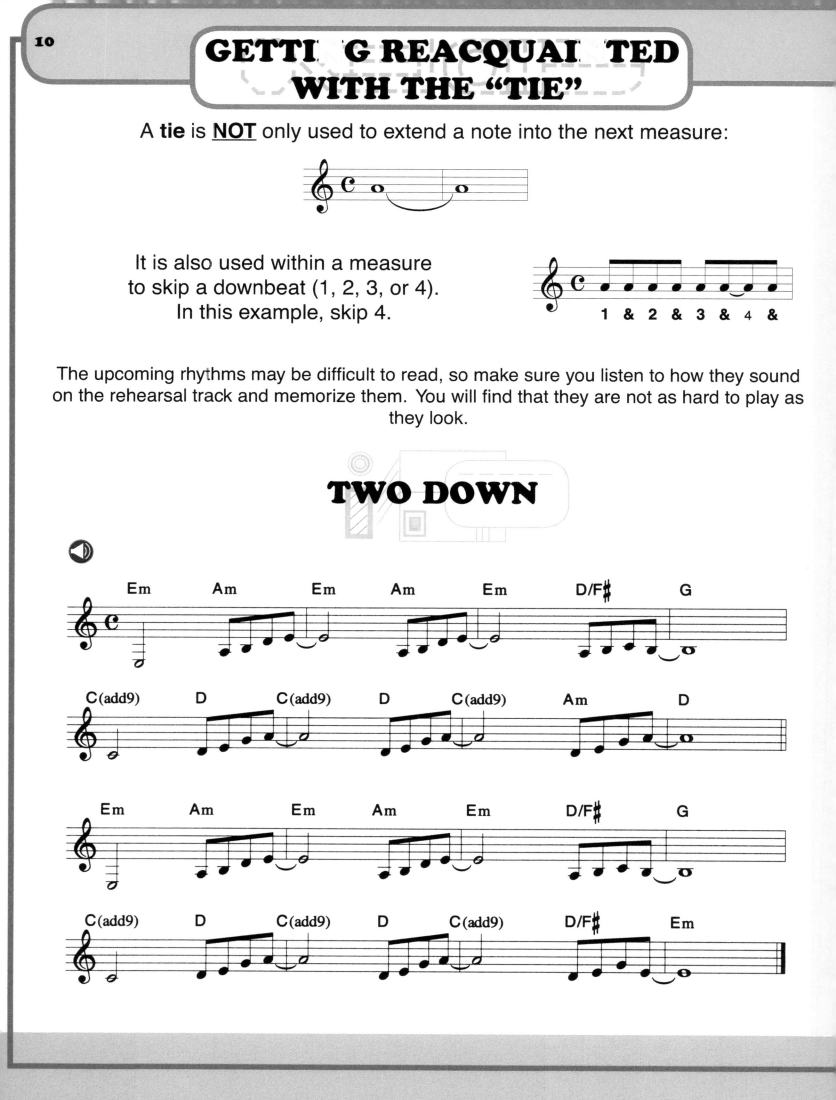

Rhythms:

Notice that beat 4 is not played because of the tie.

Remember: the dotted quarter note =1 1/2 beats.

1 & 2 & 3 & 4 &

1 & 2 & 3 & 4 &

BESIEGED

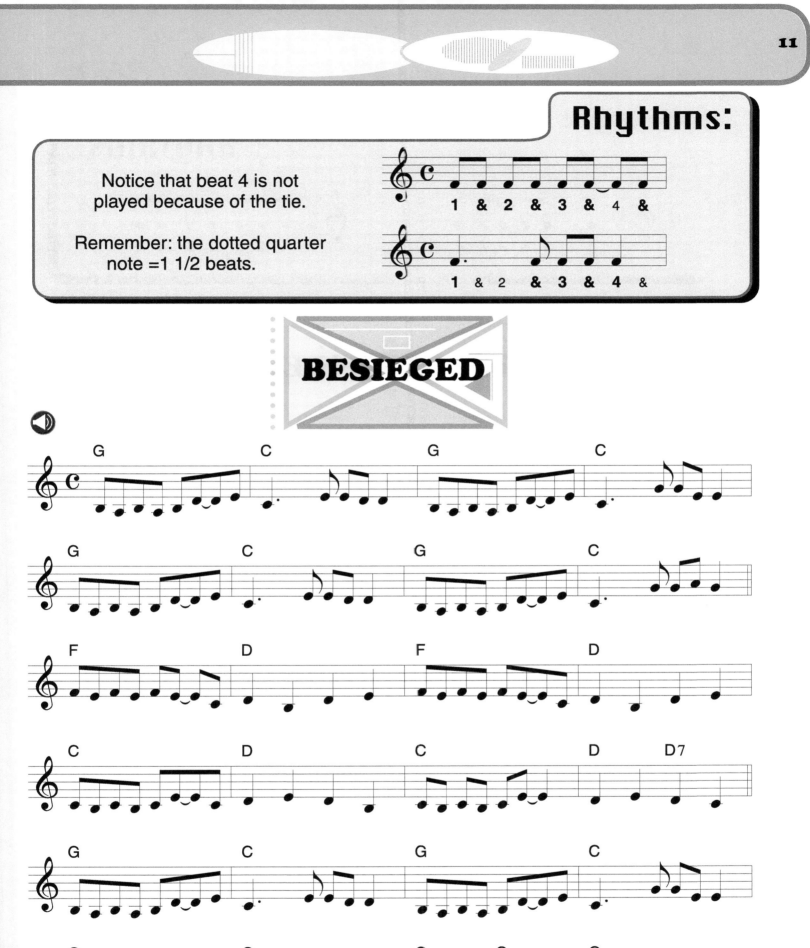

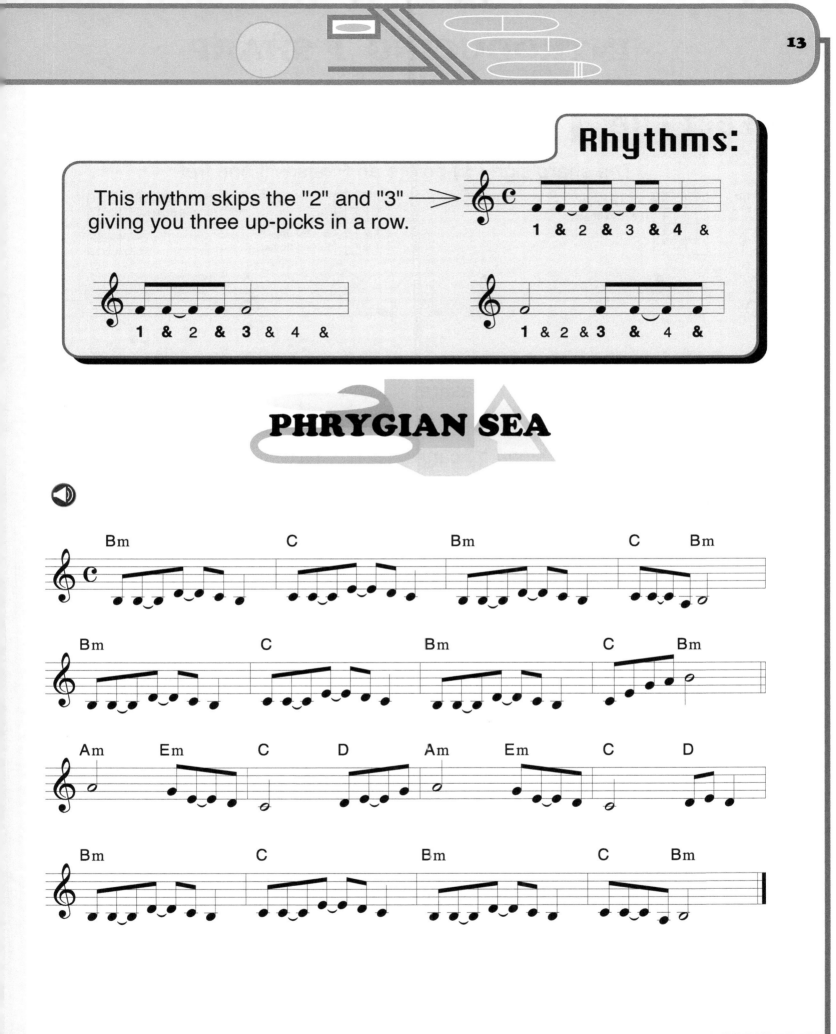

INTRODUCING F SHARP

Fact File

The sharp sign (♯) before an F raises it one fret.

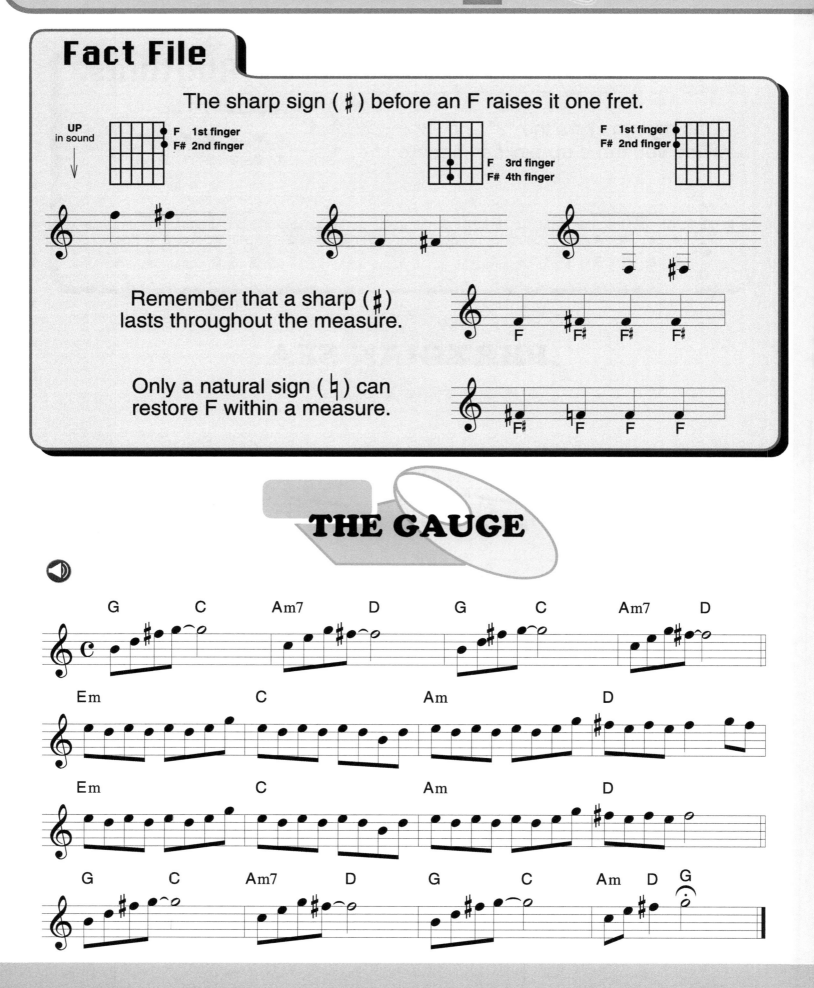

UP in sound ↓

F 1st finger
F♯ 2nd finger

F 3rd finger
F♯ 4th finger

F 1st finger
F♯ 2nd finger

Remember that a sharp (♯) lasts throughout the measure.

F   F♯   F♯   F♯

Only a natural sign (♮) can restore F within a measure.

F♯   F   F   F

THE GAUGE

| G | C | Am7 | D | G | C | Am7 | D |

| Em | C | Am | D |

| Em | C | Am | D |

| G | C | Am7 | D | G | C | Am | D | G |

Rhythms:

Like the **tie**, the **eighth rest** can also be used to skip a downbeat (1,2,3 or 4).

Example of skipping *beat 1* and *beat 3*:

(1) & 2 & (3) & 4 &

Example of skipping *beat 2* and *beat 4*:

1 & (2) & 3 & (4) &

A *rest* is not as smooth sounding as the *tie* because during the rest, the string is *muted*. The easiest way to do this is to let up on the note being played while still lightly touching the string. When resting after an open note, lightly touch the string with any finger.

ICE AGE

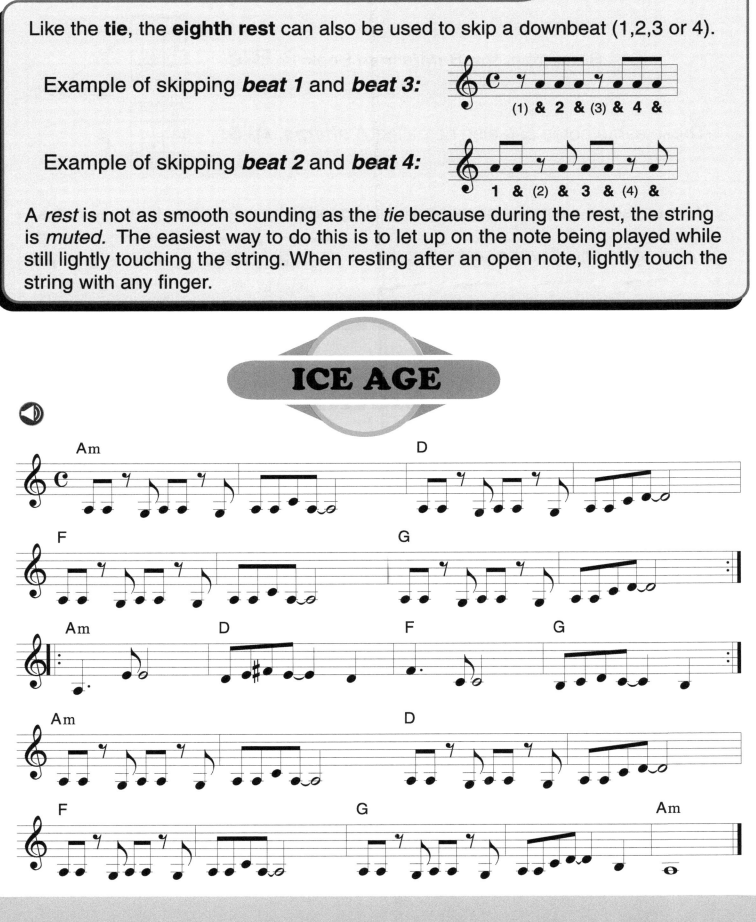

INTRODUCING A SHARP (A♯)

Fact File

Remember the *B flats* from Book 1? **B♭'s**

These same notes can also be called *A sharps.* **A♯'s**

same notes

Here are some examples showing why it is good to have 2 names for these notes.

hard to read   easy to read   hard to read   easy to read

SPARE

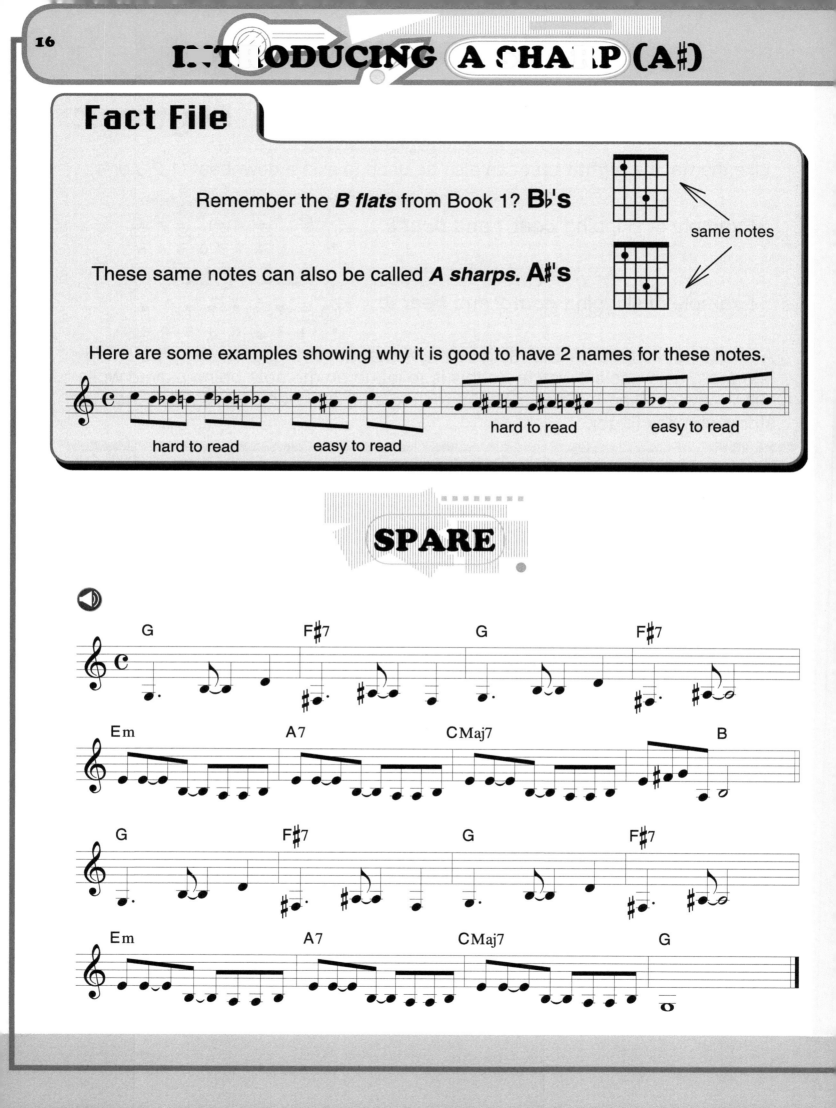

Some songs have a note that is sharp or flat throughout the entire piece. Instead of having a ♯ or ♭ in front of the note in every measure, there is a way to signify that all *F's* (for example) are sharp in a song.

The **key signature** appears at the beginning of a song between the clef sign (𝄞) and the time signature (𝄴).

The Key of G:

The ♯ on the top line (the F line) tells you that all *F's* (any octave) are *sharp* throughout the song. Only a natural sign can cancel the sharp within a measure.

The G Major Scale (2 octaves)

(F♯)   (F♯) (F♯)   (F♯)

The Key of F:

The ♭ on the middle line (the B line) tells you that all *B's* (any octave) are *flat* throughout the song. Only a natural sign can cancel the flat within a measure.

The F Major Scale (2 octaves)

(B♭)   (B♭)   (B♭)   (B♭)

The Key of C:

The key of C has *no* flats or sharps.

The C Major Scale (1 octave)

The next song is in the key of G.
This means that all notes appearing to be "F" are really "F#",
unless preceded by a natural sign (♮) in the same measure.

Fact File

Just as the 8th note is just as fast as the quarter note,
the 16th note is twice as fast as the 8th note.

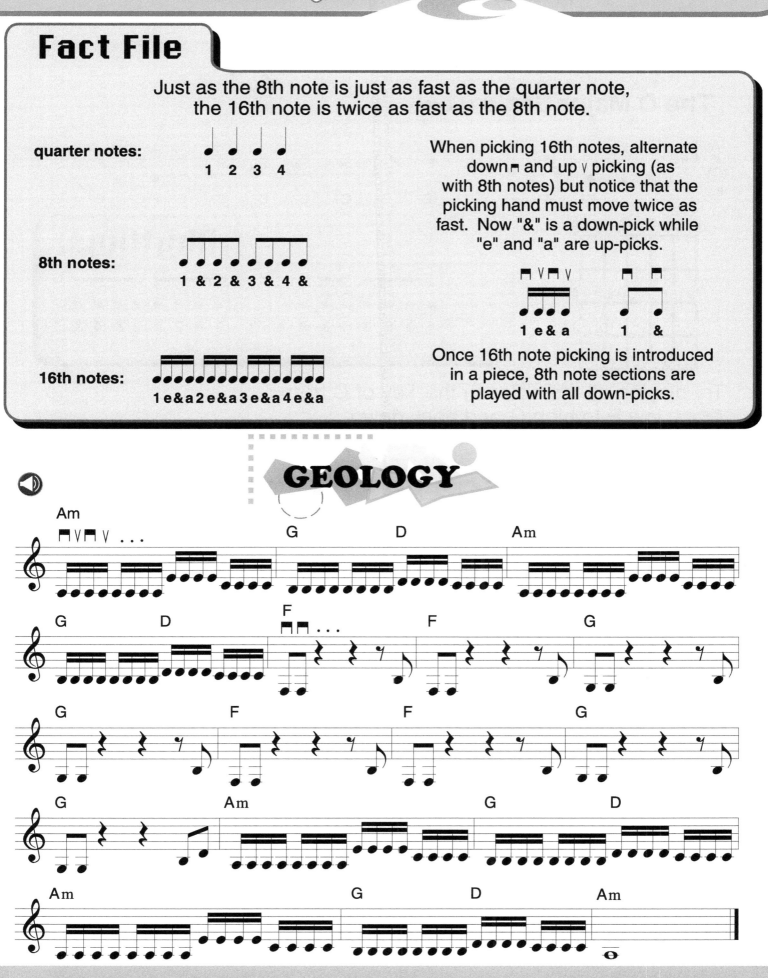

quarter notes:

1 2 3 4

When picking 16th notes, alternate down ⊓ and up ∨ picking (as with 8th notes) but notice that the picking hand must move twice as fast. Now "&" is a down-pick while "e" and "a" are up-picks.

8th notes:

1 & 2 & 3 & 4 &

1 e & a   1 &

16th notes:

1 e & a 2 e & a 3 e & a 4 e & a

Once 16th note picking is introduced in a piece, 8th note sections are played with all down-picks.

GEOLOGY

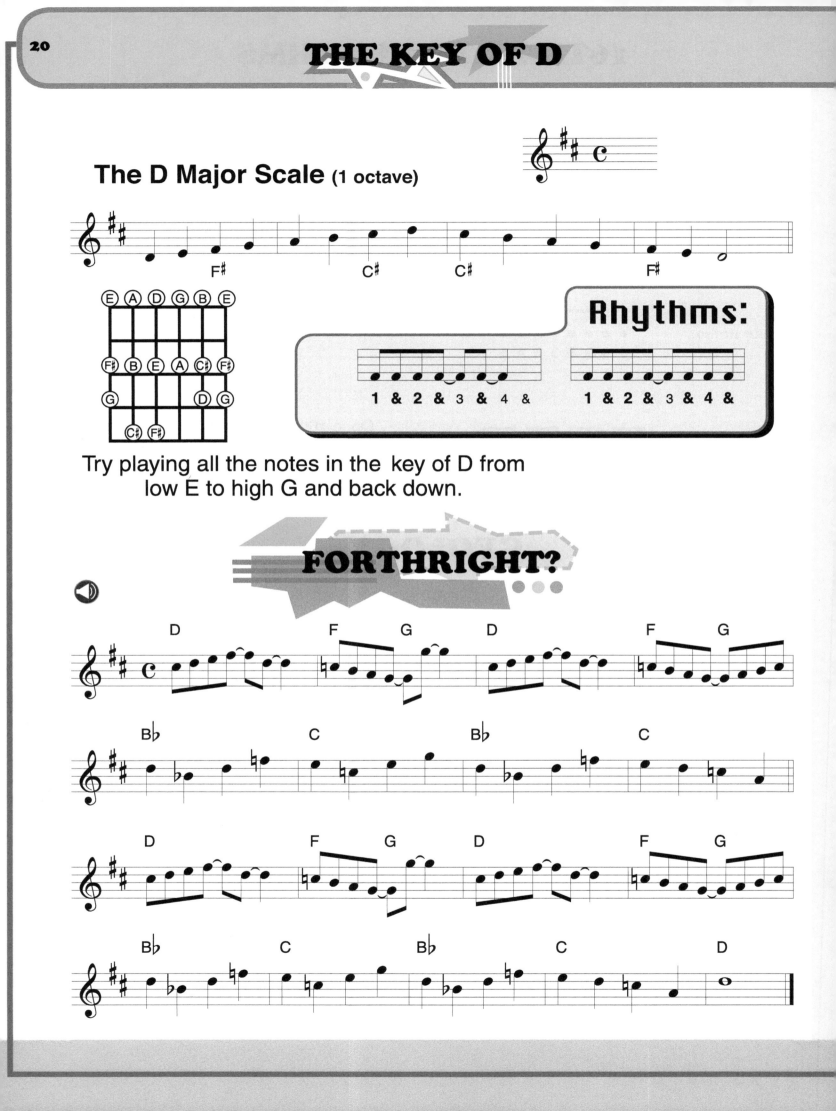

The D Major Scale (1 octave)

Try playing all the notes in the key of D from
low E to high G and back down.

Rhythms:

1 & 2 & 3 & 4 &   1 & 2 & 3 & 4 &

FORTHRIGHT?

D minor (Dm) has the same key signature as F Major (F). In fact, every major key has a "relative" minor key with the same key signature.

Rhythms:

(x..............) placed beneath a note tells you to hold that note and continue to *let it ring* to the end of the dots.

DELIVERY

PULL-OFFS

The first rhythm has a **SLUR** over the last two notes. In this case, *PULL* the 1st finger *OFF* the "F" letting the "E" ring without plucking "E". A **PULL-OFF** is one way to play a **SLUR.**

Rhythms:

pull-off

1 & 2 & 3 & 4 & a   1 & 2 & 3 & 4 &   1 e &a (2) & 3 e &a 4 &

STAIRCASE

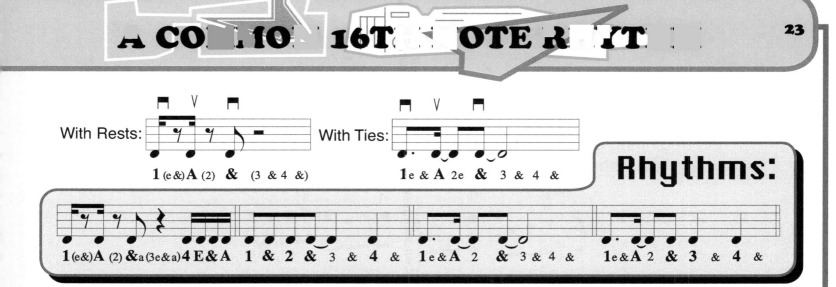

With Rests: 1 (e &) A (2) & (3 & 4 &)

With Ties: 1 e & A 2 e & 3 & 4 &

Rhythms:

1 (e &) A (2) & a (3 e & a) 4 E & A   1 & 2 & 3 & 4 &   1 e & A 2 & 3 & 4 &   1 e & A 2 & 3 & 4 &

PENTATONIC

One thing that can make a piece of music sound more *"solo"istic* is the use of repeated *patterns*. Notice that the same (4 note) pattern is repeated 4 times in the beginning of this song, except starting a note higher each time. This is a commonly used idea when playing a *solo* on any instrument.

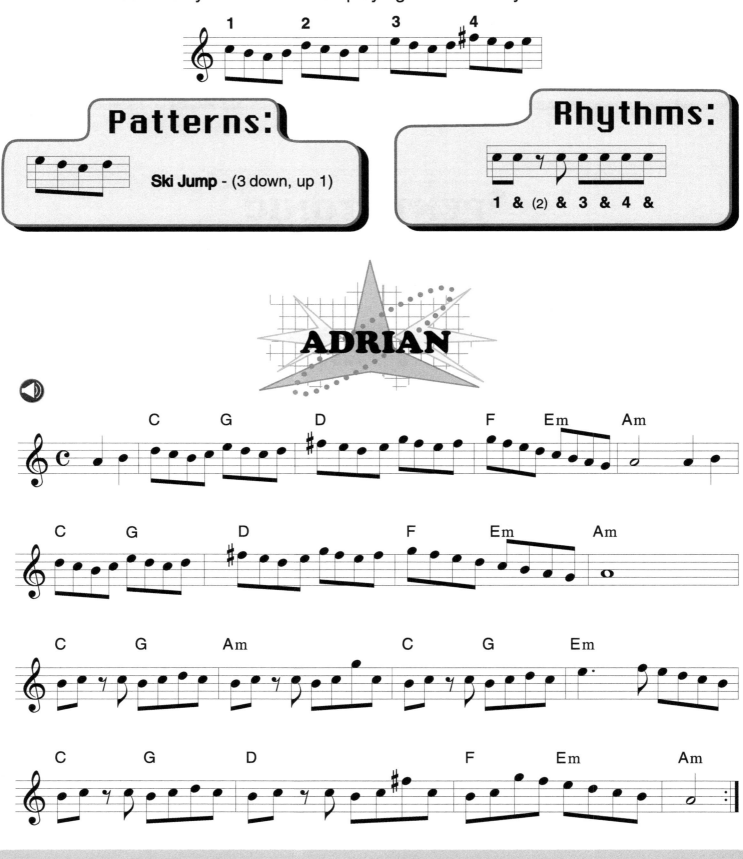

Patterns:

Ski Jump - (3 down, up 1)

Rhythms:

1 & (2) & 3 & 4 &

ADRIAN

Patterns:

4 Down - (down, down, down) **Snake -** (up, down, skip up) **Big Hill -** (up, up, down, down)

OUT ON A LEDGER

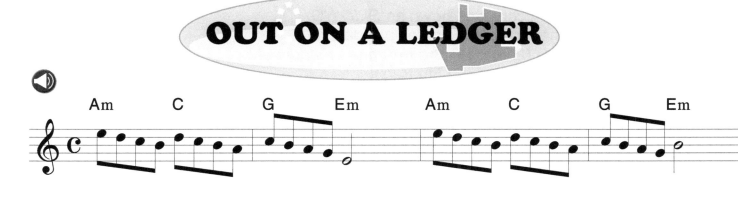

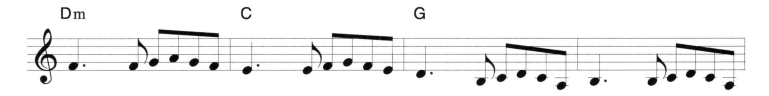

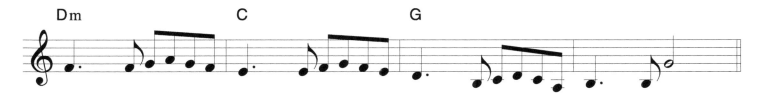

SLIDING INTO 3RD

Fact File

Playing in **3rd position** - move entire left hand up 3 frets so that the 1st finger plays on the 3rd fret, 2nd finger on the 4th, 3rd finger on the 5th, and 4th finger on the 6th fret. *REMEMBER:* Notes do not change, just the fingers that play them.

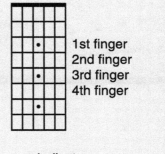

1st finger
2nd finger
3rd finger
4th finger

Measures 3 & 4 require a technique known as *SLIDING*.
• The small line before the 1st note indicates a slide into E.
• This is done by playing D (2nd string 3rd fret) and *immediately* sliding up 2 frets to the E on the 5th fret. (so immediate that D is not really heard)
• The next 2 notes (G and D) are now played with the 1st finger.
• The last E is played open (to bring you back to open position).

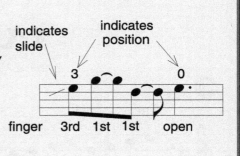

indicates slide   indicates position

finger   3rd   1st   1st   open

5TH WHEEL

Fact File

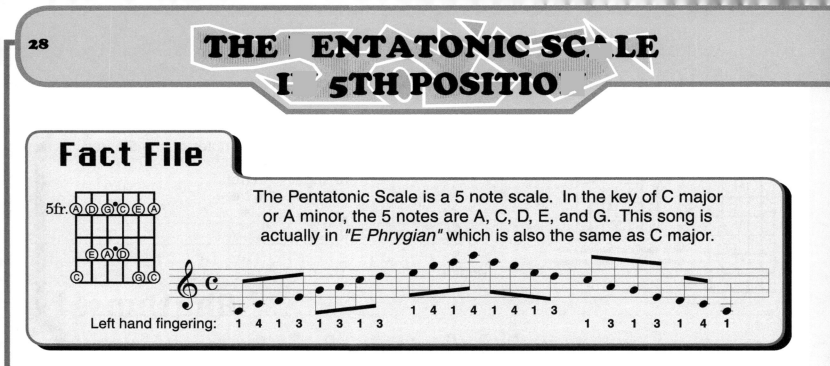

The Pentatonic Scale is a 5 note scale. In the key of C major or A minor, the 5 notes are A, C, D, E, and G. This song is actually in *"E Phrygian"* which is also the same as C major.

Left hand fingering: 1 4 1 3 1 3 1 3   1 4 1 4 1 4 1 3   1 3 1 3 1 4 1

Don't freak out! There are only 10 notes used in this entire piece.

ROCK-E VI

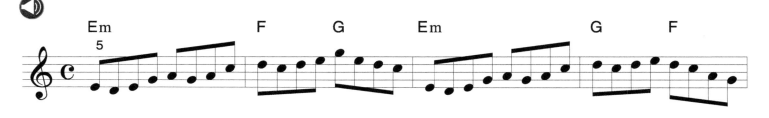

Fact File

When a repeated section of music has 2 different endings, it looks like this:

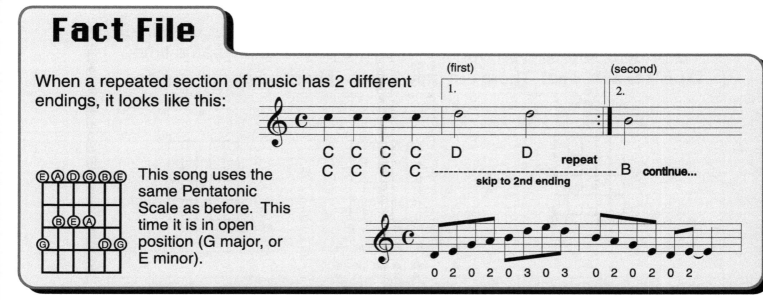

This song uses the same Pentatonic Scale as before. This time it is in open position (G major, or E minor).

SURF STRING

HARMONIZING THE E PENTATONIC SCALE

Fact File

A *Harmony* is produced when 2 notes are played at the same time.

Don't freak out! There are only 3 sets of harmonies in this piece.

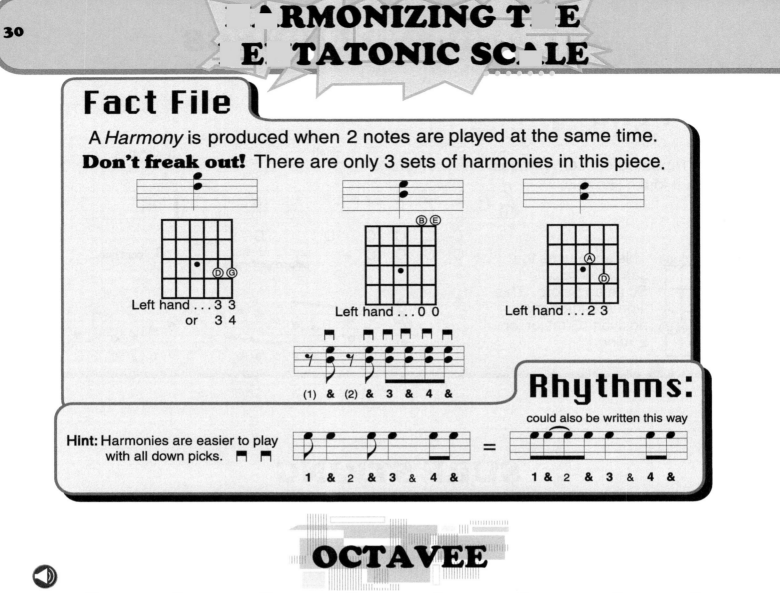

Left hand ... 3 3
or 3 4

Left hand ... 0 0

Left hand ... 2 3

(1) & (2) & 3 & 4 &

Rhythms:

could also be written this way

Hint: Harmonies are easier to play with all down picks.

1 & 2 & 3 & 4 & = 1 & 2 & 3 & 4 &

OCTAVEE

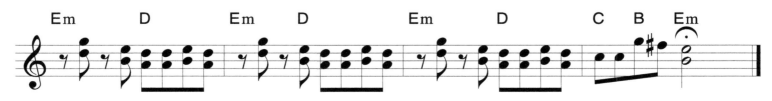

ROAMING PENTATONICS

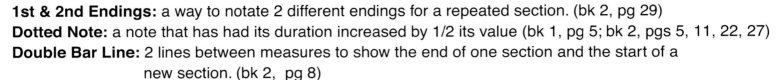

GLOSSARY

1st & 2nd Endings: a way to notate 2 different endings for a repeated section. (bk 2, pg 29)

Dotted Note: a note that has had its duration increased by 1/2 its value (bk 1, pg 5; bk 2, pgs 5, 11, 22, 27)

Double Bar Line: 2 lines between measures to show the end of one section and the start of a new section. (bk 2, pg 8)

8th Note: a note with a duration of a 1/2 beat. It takes two 8th notes to make 1 beat. (bk 1, pgs 5, 12, 18; bk 2, pgs 6,19)

Fermata: a sign that indicates a pause in time. (bk 1, pg 19)

Flat: a symbol that when placed in front of a note lowers it by 1/2 step (1 fret). (bk 1, pg 16; bk 2, pgs 16, 21, 31)

Harmony: 2 notes played at the same time. (bk 2, pg 30)

Key Signature: the sharps or flats at the beginning of a staff between the clef and the time signature indicating the key of the piece. (bk 2, pgs 17, 20, 21, 28, 29)

Ledger Lines: short lines above or below the staff for higher or lower notes. (bk 1, pg 23; 27, 30; bk 2, pg 4)

Major Scale: a 7 note scale that includes all the notes in a major key. (bk 2, pgs 17, 20)

Minor Scale: a 7 note scale that includes all the notes in a minor key. (bk 1, pg 27; bk 2, pg 21)

Natural Sign: a symbol that cancels a sharp or flat for the rest of that measure. (bk 1, pg 16; bk 2, pgs 14,16-18, 20-23)

Octave: a lower or higher version of the same note. (bk 1, pg 30; bk 2, pgs 14,16,17)

Open: any of the 6 strings played without pressing a fret. (bk 1, pgs 4, 6, 14, 20, 24; bk 2, pgs 15, 26, 29, 31)

Pattern: a grouping of notes in some type of recognizable order. (bk 1, pg 7; bk 2, pgs 7, 9, 24, 25)

Pentatonic Scale: a 5 note version of the major scale, leaving out the 4th & 7th notes. (bk 2, pgs 28-31)

Position: the fret that the first finger is assigned to play for a section of music. (3rd fret = 3rd position, 5th fret = 5th position). If there are open notes this is called open position. (bk 2, pgs 26, 29, 31)

Pull-off: the technique of pulling a finger off the fret after plucking a note and allowing the next note to ring without being plucked. (bk 2, pg 22)

Relative Minor: the minor key that has the same key signature as a particular major key. (bk 2, pg 21)

Repeat Signs: signs that mean to play a section of music again. (bk 1, pgs 19, 31; bk 2, pgs 24, 26, 29-31)

Rest: a beat of silence (length determined by type of rest) (bk 1, pg 18, 23, 26, 31; bk 2, pgs 15, 18, 19, 21-24, 30)

Rhythm: the beat pattern that a group of notes has due to the different types of notes used in the measure such as; half, quarter, 8th,etc. (bk 2, pgs 11-13, 18-24, 27, 30)

Sharp: a symbol that when placed in front of a note raises it by 1/2 step (1 fret). (bk 2, pgs 14,16-18, 20, 22-24, 30)

Sixteenth Note: a note with a duration of 1/4 beat. It takes four 16th notes to make 1 beat. (bk 2, pgs 5,19, 21-23, 27)

Slide: a technique of plucking a fretted note then sliding the finger to a different fret and allowing the new note (and any note in between) to sound without plucking. (bk 2, pgs 26, 31)

Slur: a curved line connecting two different notes indicating the second is not plucked. A slide pull-off or other technique is used. (bk 2, pgs 22, 26, 31)

Tie: a curved line connecting two notes of the same pitch, allowing the note to ring for its value plus that of the second note, which is not played. (bk 1, pg 22; bk 2, pgs 4, 10-16, 18, 20-23, 25-27, 29)